THE SAN FRANCISCO EARTHQUAKE AND FIRE

by Chrös McDougall

Content Consultant
Rodger C. Birt, PhD
Professor Emeritus, College of Humanities
San Francisco State University

CORE
LIBRARY

Published by ABDO Publishing Company, PO Box 398166, Minneapolis, MN 55439. Copyright © 2014 by Abdo Consulting Group, Inc. International copyrights reserved in all countries. No part of this book may be reproduced in any form without written permission from the publisher. The Core Library™ is a trademark and logo of ABDO Publishing Company.

Printed in the United States of America, North Mankato, Minnesota
042013
112013

♻ THIS BOOK CONTAINS AT LEAST 10% RECYCLED MATERIALS.

Editor: Blythe Hurley
Series Designer: Becky Daum

Library of Congress Control Number: 2013932004

Cataloging-in-Publication Data
McDougall, Chros.
 The San Francisco earthquake and fire / Chros McDougall.
  p. cm. -- (History's greatest disasters)
ISBN 978-1-61783-959-7 (lib. bdg.)
ISBN 978-1-62403-024-6 (pbk.)
Includes bibliographical references and index.
1. Earthquakes--California--San Francisco Bay Area--Juvenile literature. 2. Fires--California--San Francisco Bay Area--Juvenile literature.   I. Title.
363.34--dc23

                                                2013932004

Photo Credits: Library of Congress, cover, 1; AP Images, 4, 7, 10, 17, 19, 25, 28, 32, 45; U.S. Geological Survey/AP Images, 9; James Balog/Getty Images, 12; Red Line Editorial, Inc., 16, 29; Bettmann/Corbis/AP Images, 21, 22, 27, 36, 40; San Francisco Public Library/AP Images, 34; John Swart/AP Images, 39

CONTENTS

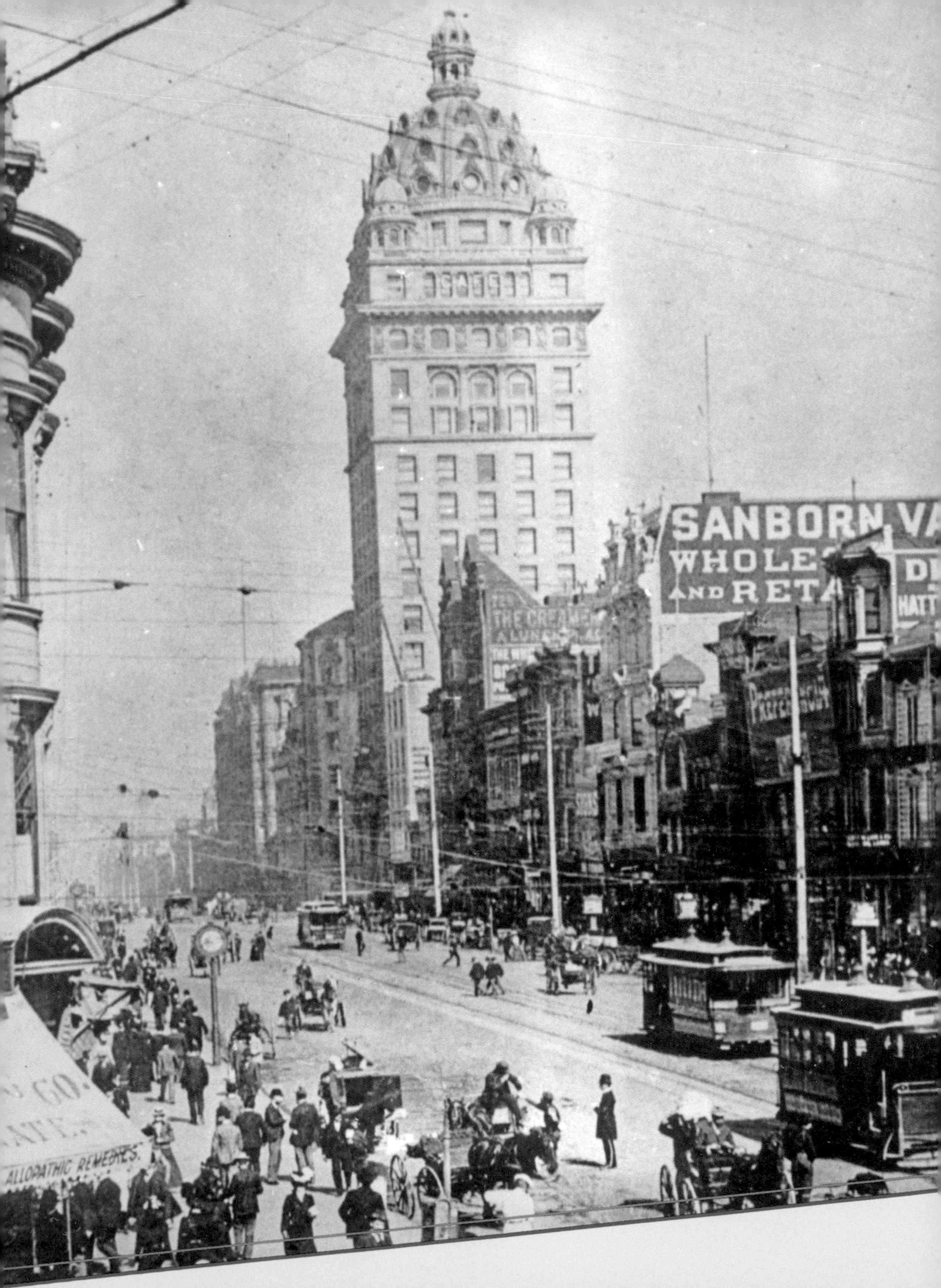
SANBORN VA
WHOLE
AND RETA
ALLOPATHIC REMEDIES

CHAPTER ONE

THE EARTH SHAKES

The streets of the United States' greatest western city were just beginning to stir on Wednesday, April 18, 1906. It should have been a morning like any other in San Francisco, California.

It was still dark when the city's famous cable cars began running at 5:00 a.m. Some early risers were on the streets. Many more San Franciscans were still in

San Francisco was the biggest city on the West Coast at the beginning of the 1900s.

San Francisco

Today the San Francisco Bay Area is a major urban center. There are several large cities there. These include San Francisco, San Jose, and Oakland. The Bay Area and the entire West Coast looked very different in 1906. The West Coast had only begun to grow in 1849. That year an incredible 50,000 people flocked to the Bay Area in search of gold. California became a state the next year. San Francisco was easily the biggest and most important West Coast city in 1906. The earthquake and fire changed that forever.

bed. The day that would change the city forever had just begun.

Waves of Earth

A police sergeant named Jesse B. Cook was on the street at the eastern edge of San Francisco that morning. Cook would later become the chief of police in San Francisco. He remembered hearing a deep rumble underground. He looked west down Washington Street, toward Chinatown and the Pacific Ocean.

"It was as if the waves of the ocean were coming toward me," he recalled. Cook was seeing the ground rolling in waves caused by a powerful earthquake.

This home was snapped from its foundation by the 1906 earthquake.

These waves were violently destroying the city as they moved.

The city was helpless. Buildings shook and swayed as if they were made of paper. Some buildings crumbled. Others snapped from their foundations. If the violent shaking hadn't woken everyone already, the sounds of snapping wood and tumbling chimneys certainly did.

Many San Franciscans rushed into the streets in search of safety from the falling buildings. But little safety was to be found. Bricks and stonework rained onto the streets from above. Dust and debris made it hard to see or move. Several roads buckled and formed large cracks. Many people found it impossible to escape.

The first tremors had begun at 5:12 a.m. Within a half minute, the earthquake was violently shaking San Francisco. An earthquake's shock waves lose strength as they travel. But this earthquake was so strong, its vibrations were felt as

City Hall

The 1906 earthquake destroyed structures of all kinds throughout the San Francisco area. Among these was the famous City Hall. It had taken 25 years to build. The building was one of the most famous in the American West. Yet like so many other buildings, it could not withstand the shaking. The walls quickly fell in a shower of bricks. Soon little more than the building's frame and famous 300-foot (91 m) dome remained.

The earthquake almost completely destroyed San Francisco's famous City Hall.

Survivors walk through the rubble of a destroyed section of San Francisco.

far north as Oregon and as far south as Los Angeles, California.

The worst of the earthquake probably lasted less than a minute. Yet its awesome power had left San Francisco unrecognizable. Broken water pipes and gas lines were shooting their contents up from underground. At the time this seemed to be the least of the city's problems. But those broken pipes would lead to the destruction of San Francisco.

The 1906 earthquake caused terrible damage throughout San Francisco. E. E. Schmitz, the city's mayor, wrote a letter to his citizens that the area's newspapers then printed:

> *The federal troops, which are now policing a portion of the city, as well as the regular and special members of the police force, have been authorized by me to kill any persons whomsoever found engaged in looting the effects of any citizens, or otherwise engaged in the commission of crime.*
>
> *Under these circumstances the request is made that all citizens whose business does not imperatively require their absence from home after dark, remain at home during the night or until order shall have been restored. I beg to warn all citizens of the danger of fire.*

Source: *"Fire Demon Follows Earthquake – Magnitude of Disaster Unknown."* Minneapolis Tribune *April 19, 1906. Print. 2.*

Changing Minds

Read the passage above carefully. How could you adapt Mayor Schmitz's words for a modern audience, such as your neighbors or your classmates? Write a blog post giving this same information to the new audience. What is the most effective way to get your point across to this audience? How is the language you use for the new audience different from the original text? Why?

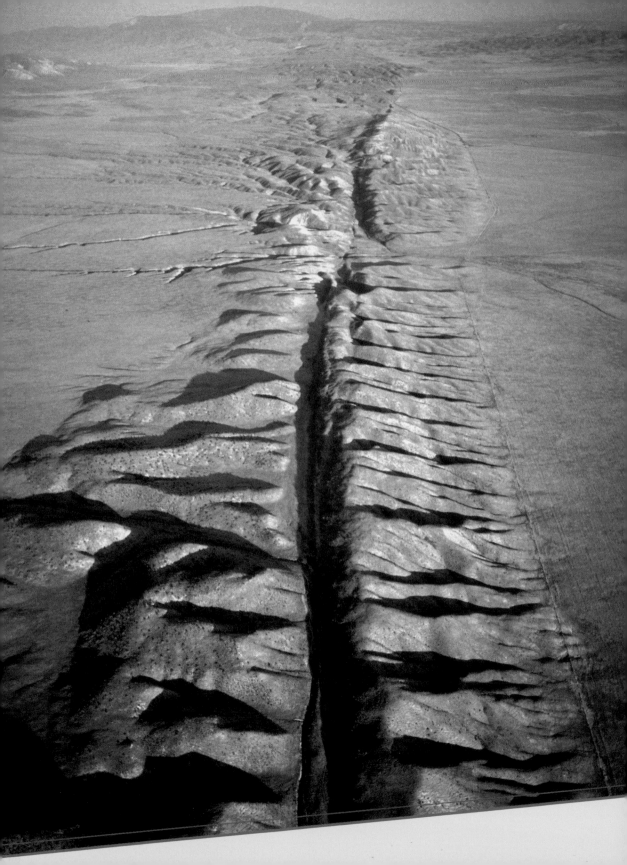

AT FAULT

Earthquakes were nothing new in the San Francisco area. Scientists estimate that earthquakes have been occurring there since the region formed 15 to 20 million years ago. In fact earthquakes happen along the California coast all the time. These quakes are usually too small for humans to feel.

The 1906 earthquake was different. Tools were not yet available to measure it by modern standards.

California frequently experiences earthquake activity because of its location on the San Andreas Fault.

Measuring Earthquakes

Today scientists measure earthquakes in two ways. Magnitude measures the size of an earthquake. Intensity measures the severity of shaking. There are different ways in which magnitude is measured. But by any measure, the 1906 earthquake was huge. Scientists believe that no earthquake in the lower 48 states has been bigger since. The 1906 earthquake was also very intense. The Modified Mercalli Intensity Scale measures intensity from I to a maximum of XII. Scientists estimate the 1906 earthquake would have measured XI. An earthquake that strong destroys most buildings, bridges, and railroads.

However, scientists believe it would have ranked among the most powerful earthquakes ever recorded.

But what causes these quakes to happen?

The Science behind Earthquakes

The earth's surface is made up of massive rock formations called tectonic plates. These plates wrap around the globe like a giant cracked eggshell. Scientists call the area where two plates meet a fault line.

Tectonic plates are always moving. Sometimes the plates get stuck. This creates a lot of force. When that force is relieved, the plates snap apart. This causes the land above one plate to pull away from the land above the other plate. This is the cause of one type of earthquake.

The 1906 earthquake occurred along the San Andreas Fault. This fault line runs for approximately 800 miles (1,287 km) along the western edge of California. In 1906 land above the San Andreas Fault slipped along approximately 270 miles (435 km) of the fault. At the worst point, the ground moved between 21 and 32 feet (6 and 10 m). Areas that had once been right next to each other were suddenly the length of a school bus apart.

Shock Waves Roll through San Francisco

The movement along the fault in San Francisco was less violent than in other areas. But the focus of the quake, which is the spot underground where a fault

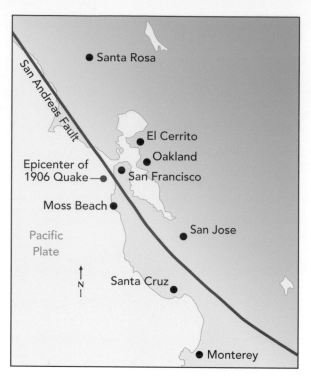

The San Andreas Fault

On April 18, 1906, the San Andreas Fault snapped near San Francisco. This diagram shows the fault's location and how close the epicenter was to San Francisco. What does this map tell you about the scale of the 1906 earthquake? How does seeing the map help you better understand the earthquake's powerful effect on San Francisco?

begins to split, was in the Pacific Ocean only two miles (3.2 km) west of San Francisco. The earthquake sent energy known as seismic waves rippling away from the focus in all directions. These waves moved as quickly as three miles (5 km) per second. A university

The earthquake flattened much of San Francisco's wealthy Nob Hill neighborhood.

in Japan recorded minor vibrations within 12 minutes of the quake!

The violent shaking caused by these shock waves hit San Francisco hard. The high intensity was in part because the epicenter of the quake was so close to the city. The epicenter is the spot on Earth's surface directly above the focus.

Earlier Quakes

San Francisco had already experienced one major earthquake in its short history. On October 21, 1868, the Hayward Fault across San Francisco Bay ruptured. Thirty people died in the quake. But by 1906, that earthquake was a distant memory for most people in busy San Francisco.

San Francisco had grown a great deal from 1868 to 1906. Approximately 400,000 people lived there. Another 250,000 people lived in the greater Bay Area. But these residents did not truly understand the moderate tremors that shook the area on occasion. And the decades without a major event had led the city to forget the lessons learned from 1868.

Unprepared

The 1906 earthquake hit a glamorous, growing city. San Francisco was more than three times bigger than the next largest city on the West Coast. It was a thriving cultural center. It boasted fancy theaters,

San Francisco was not prepared for the earthquake that nearly destroyed it in 1906.

hotels, and shops. But it was poorly prepared for an earthquake.

Many buildings, including some of the most famous ones, were structurally weak. In addition, people had built parts of the city on soft, reclaimed land. These were areas where people had created more land for the city to grow on by filling in part of San Francisco Bay with earth and garbage. These

Grand Buildings

The Call Building at 703 Market Street in San Francisco stood 15 stories and 310 feet (95 m) tall. It was San Francisco's first skyscraper. The Ferry Building at the end of Market Street stood out with its 245-foot (75-m) clock tower. The 1906 earthquake and fire badly damaged both of these buildings. But both ultimately survived. Today the Ferry Building is a popular market and transportation hub. The Call Building has changed dramatically since it was built. Its famous dome was removed in 1937, and six additional stories were added. It is now named the Central Tower.

two factors proved particularly damaging on the morning of April 18. The weak structures built on reclaimed land stood no chance. Buildings on harder soil did not do much better. Many weak, wood-framed buildings in such areas shook so hard their bricks fell off. Structures snapped from their foundations. In less than three minutes, San Francisco had been turned to ruins.

Soldiers walk east along Market Street after the earthquake. The Call Building, with its distinctive dome, can be seen burning in the background.

EXPLORE ONLINE

Chapter Two talks about what causes earthquakes. The Web site below has lots of information about earthquakes too. As you know, every source is different. How is the information given in this Web site different from the information in this chapter? What information is the same? How do the two sources present information differently? What can you learn from this Web site?

The Science of Earthquakes

www.mycorelibrary.com/san-francisco-earthquake

CHAPTER THREE

EVERYTHING BURNS

The immediate aftermath of the earthquake was grim. Buildings were left in ruins from San Francisco all the way down the peninsula to San Jose, 45 miles (72 km) south. The first aftershock shook the city shortly after the earthquake. An aftershock is a small earthquake that occurs in the same area after the main quake. Approximately

A massive cloud of smoke rises from San Francisco as flames devour the city after the 1906 earthquake.

Bay Area Tragedies

San Francisco was the city hit hardest by the earthquake and fires. But smaller cities lower on the peninsula also suffered serious property damage and loss of lives. One of the many tragedies caused by the earthquake happened at the Agnews State Hospital for the Insane near San Jose. Hundreds of patients were crammed into weak brick buildings there. The buildings crumbled during the earthquake. This disaster killed at least 110 people. It was the largest recorded death toll caused by the earthquake in one place.

15 minutes later, there were reports of nearly 50 fires in downtown San Francisco.

A New Level of Destruction

A nightmare quickly began throughout San Francisco. Firefighters rushed to stop the fires only to find no running water. The earthquake had broken the city's main water pipes, called water mains. The city's water was gushing up through cracks in the streets. Meanwhile, broken underground gas lines spewed flammable gas into the air. Fires broke out everywhere.

Residents watch as smoke and fire spread through the city after the earthquake.

Those people who were not trapped under rubble scrambled to find safety. But there was little safety to be found. And just after 8:00 a.m., another aftershock shook the city. Some buildings that had been left barely standing by the main quake fell.

The worst of the earthquake was now over. But the fire, which was even more destructive, was just beginning.

The Army Takes Control

Army General Frederick Funston took control of San Francisco early Wednesday morning. Funston ordered troops into the city. The soldiers' job was to keep order and help firefighters. Most displaced civilians were well behaved. That might have been due in part to Funston's hard line on troublemakers. He ordered that thieves be immediately shot dead. As a result, a handful of people were shot and killed for causing trouble.

Fires Take the City

The fire began as dozens of small blazes. Some of them likely started when sparks from fallen electrical lines ignited leaking gas. Others might have been started by everyday fires that were already burning before the quake, such as in cooking stoves and fireplaces. Soon all of these smaller fires began to combine to form larger and larger blazes.

Wind helped the fires spread. So did the way in which the city was built. Many people and businesses had moved to San Francisco in the decades before

While this fire crew was able to put out the fire in San Francisco's Mission District, firefighters were unable to stop many of the city's blazes.

the earthquake. To keep up with the demand for buildings, the city had allowed people to build many cheap wooden structures. Those buildings were generally the first to crumble during the earthquake. Then they were the first to go up in flames afterward. Fire quickly spread throughout the city.

The Blaze Takes Over

With little running water, firefighters and soldiers had few defenses against the flames. The fire spread quickly from building to building. It jumped

Damaged roads made leaving the city difficult for survivors.

across streets. Firefighters tried blowing up outlying buildings with dynamite. The goal was to create a gap that the fire would not be able to cross. This was more effective in some places than in others. Sometimes untrained firefighters misused the dynamite. This accidentally created even more fires.

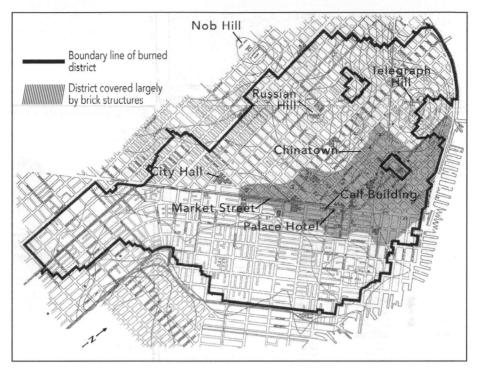

Areas Damaged by the Fire

The 1906 earthquake caused terrible damage to San Francisco. But the resulting fire is what truly destroyed the city. The area outlined in red in the map above indicates parts of the city that were almost completely destroyed by the fire. Fire damaged 28,188 buildings over 4.7 square miles (12 sq km). After reading about the fire, how large did you imagine it was? How does seeing the area damaged by the fire help you to better understand the destruction it caused?

Those people not fighting the fires had few safe places to go. The earthquake had destroyed most homes. The fires that continued through Thursday and Friday destroyed many parts of the city that had survived the earthquake.

Ways out of the city were limited. Some people were able to take ferries across the bay to Oakland. But many San Franciscans were unable to leave the city. News reports estimated that the disaster left approximately 200,000 people homeless. Some stayed in tents at refugee camps in city parks. Others simply found open spaces throughout the city. They waited with little available food or water for the fires to be put out.

Finally, on Saturday, April 21, there was nothing left for the fire to burn. A rain shower put out the last flames. After a few minutes of shaking and several days of fires, more than 28,000 buildings had been destroyed. More than half of the city's 400,000 residents were left homeless. And it is believed that approximately 3,000 people died.

Now it was time to start rebuilding America's greatest western city.

In 1906 writer and historian Marshall Everett wrote a book about the San Francisco earthquake and fire. In one section, Everett describes the scene as fire spread through the city on the evening of April 18:

> As the flames spread into the residence districts people left their homes and fled to the parks and squares.
>
> The city resembled one vast shambles with the red glare of the fire throwing weird shadows across the worn and panic-stricken faces of the homeless wandering the streets or sleeping on piles of mattresses and clothing in the parks and on the sidewalks in those districts not yet reached by the fire.

Source: Marshall Everett. Complete Story of the San Francisco Earthquake. *Chicago: The Bible House, 1906. Print. 50.*

Back It Up

In the passage above, Everett uses descriptive language to make a point. What point do you think he is trying to make? Write a paragraph describing the point you think he is making. Then write down two or three pieces of evidence he uses to make that point.

CHAPTER FOUR

NEW BEGINNINGS

Fires were still burning in San Francisco when people began to talk about rebuilding. "In my opinion, San Francisco in a few years will be a greater and grander city than it ever was before," one resident told the *New York Times* newspaper on April 20.

That positive attitude among citizens helped in the rebuilding efforts. Many postal workers kept

Many earthquake survivors took up temporary residence in refugees camps such as this one.

All JEWELRY and DIAMOND PLEDGES left with us are perfectly safe and secure as we are the only LOAN OFFICE West of Chicago that has its own FIRE & BURGLAR PROOF VAULTS on premises

PORTLAND JEWELRY CO. 22-25 STOCKTON ST

WHY?

MADE PEOPLE HAPPY

ADS

A business displays a sign reassuring customers that their valuables could be stored there after the disaster.

working through the disaster. They found ways to allow people to send and receive mail despite the tragedy. And the strongly built mint, where the government made and stored coins and paper money, survived in working order. That helped banks and other businesses get back up and running quickly.

Rebuilding the City by the Bay

The people of San Francisco wanted to rebuild the city quickly. The government and businesses encouraged people to stay and to keep moving there. The new San Francisco that appeared looked different. Few buildings or landmarks from before 1906 were still there.

San Francisco was still an important city. But the events of 1906 did cause a major change for the city by the bay. Many people now understood San Francisco would always be vulnerable to earthquakes. People and business owners began looking elsewhere to set down roots.

Workers repair telegraph wires amid the rubble of the earthquake and fire.

West Coast cities such as Los Angeles, Seattle, and Portland more than doubled in size from 1900 to 1910. Los Angeles topped San Francisco as the largest West Coast city during the 1910s. San Francisco's population has also more than doubled since 1906. Today more than 7 million people live in the greater Bay Area. But the 1906 earthquake and fire ensured that San Francisco would no longer be the biggest West Coast city. Los Angeles now holds that title with more than 10 million residents in the area.

Understanding Earthquakes

The 1906 earthquake and fire combined to cause a natural disaster unlike any the United States had seen before. Scientists and government officials began searching for its causes. The government's findings about the 1906 earthquake appeared in a

Chinatown

Chinatown is a unique San Francisco neighborhood. This area in the heart of San Francisco has been home to Chinese immigrants since 1848. However, the earthquake and fire destroyed the neighborhood in 1906. Many white people in San Francisco saw this as a chance to move Chinatown to a less desirable part of the city. But China's government and a wealthy Chinese-American businessman made sure that did not happen. Chinatown was rebuilt at its original location just north of Market Street. Today this lively neighborhood still celebrates Chinese culture.

Elastic Rebound Theory

Research done after the 1906 earthquake helped scientists better understand what happened in San Francisco. One important finding was the theory of elastic rebound. This theory explains that rocks beneath the earth's surface strain at the fault lines. This strain causes these rocks to change shape. When the strain becomes too much, the rocks snap back to their original shapes, like a plucked guitar string. That snapping motion is what causes earthquakes. Most scientists still accept this theory.

publication called the *Lawson Report* two years later. This research was the beginning of modern earthquake science.

Earthquake science is still not exact. Scientists cannot accurately predict when and where an earthquake will happen. But research and better tools have made places such as San Francisco safer. Scientists now know where earthquakes could possibly take place. This allows cities to better prepare. For example, cities now avoid building on fault lines or on soft soil. In addition, new standards ensure that buildings and infrastructure are much

Police officers escort a woman through the rubble of her destroyed Marina District apartment after the 1989 earthquake in San Francisco.

stronger. Infrastructure is the basic systems that serve the public. This includes roads, railroads, water pipes, and electricity lines.

An earthquake tested the Bay Area once again in 1989. On October 17, a major earthquake happened along the San Andreas Fault at Loma Prieta

These cars were destroyed by the 1989 quake.

peak, approximately 60 miles (97 km) south of San Francisco. It was the first major earthquake to hit the Bay Area since 1906.

The 1906 earthquake was stronger and had an epicenter closer to San Francisco. But the 1989 earthquake still hit the Bay Area hard. Sixty-three people died in this quake. Several older buildings and structures built on reclaimed land fell. Some

FURTHER EVIDENCE

There is a lot of information in Chapter Four about the changes that have happened in San Francisco since 1906. This chapter also talks about the many discoveries that have been made in earthquake science since that time. What do you think the main point of this chapter is? What key evidence supports that point? Check out the Web site at the link below. Can you find a quote on the Web site that supports the author's point? Now write a few sentences using information from the Web site as evidence to support the main point of this chapter.

Earthquake Science

www.mycorelibrary.com/san-francisco-earthquake

infrastructure failed as well. The earthquake even forced the World Series between the San Francisco Giants and the Oakland Athletics to be postponed.

But this disaster did not approach the size of the 1906 earthquake and fire. And once again, San Francisco and the Bay Area recovered. Today the area is safer. It is still one of the greatest cities both on the West Coast and in the world.

1849

Thousands of people flock to San Francisco, California, in search of gold, beginning the city's period as the largest city on the West Coast.

1850

California becomes the thirty-first state to join the United States.

1868

The first major earthquake to hit a settled San Francisco occurs on October 21, when the Hayward Fault ruptures across San Francisco Bay. Thirty people die.

1906

Fire continues to destroy San Francisco on Thursday and Friday, April 19 and 20.

1906

After more than three days of burning, the great fire finally dies out on Saturday, April 21.

1908

The US government releases the *Lawson Report*, creating the foundation for future earthquake research.

1906

A massive earthquake wakes San Franciscans at 5:12 a.m. on Wednesday, April 18. The epicenter is just two miles (3.2 km) west of San Francisco.

1906

General Frederick Funston assumes control of San Francisco early in the morning on Wednesday, April 18.

1906

By midday on April 18, fires raging in central San Francisco destroy prominent buildings.

1910s

Los Angeles replaces San Francisco as the largest US city on the West Coast.

1937

The Call Building's dome is removed and six additional floors are added.

1989

The Loma Prieta earthquake hits the San Francisco Bay Area on October 17. It is the first major earthquake to hit the area since 1906.

Why Do I Care?

The San Francisco earthquake and fire happened more than a century ago. But there are good reasons why people still talk about those events today. How might the 1906 earthquake and fire have affected your life? What safety measures are in place today that might not have been in place in 1906? How might history be different had the 1906 earthquake and fire happened in a less populated area?

Take a Stand

Due to the San Andreas Fault, the San Francisco area will always be at risk for earthquakes. Yet people rebuilt San Francisco and continued moving to the Bay Area after 1906. Was it right for people to rebuild San Francisco? Or should the survivors have made a new city somewhere safer? Write a short essay explaining your opinion. Make sure to give reasons for your opinion, and facts and details that support those reasons.

You Are There

Imagine that you awoke at 5:12 a.m. on April 18, 1906, to find your city crumbling around you. What would you do? Would you know the safest place to go? Write a 300-word letter to your family about your experiences. Be sure to include how you felt about each event you describe.

Say What?

Studying earthquakes can mean learning a lot of new vocabulary. Find five words in this book that you've never heard before. Use a dictionary to find out what they mean. Then write the meanings in your own words, and use each word in a sentence.

GLOSSARY

aftershock
a small earthquake that occurs in the same area after the main earthquake

epicenter
the point on the earth's surface directly above an earthquake's focus

fault
the place where two tectonic plates come together and where earthquakes begin

focus
the spot underground where an earthquake fault begins to rupture

force
power or energy

reclaimed land
areas that used to be part of a body of water that people have filled in with earth or debris, usually in order to expand coastal cities

refugee camp
a place where people who have nowhere else to go can stay, usually during a crisis

rupture
to break apart

seismic waves
waves of energy that travel through the earth's core during an earthquake

tectonic plates
large rocks beneath the earth's surface that form together to cover the entire globe

LEARN MORE

Books

Burkhart, David. *Earthquake Days: The 1906 San Francisco Earthquake & Fire in 3-D*. San Bruno, CA: Faultline Books, 2005.

Jeffers, H. Paul. *Disaster by the Bay*. Guilford, CT: Lyons Press, 2003.

Winchester, Simon. *A Crack in the Edge of the World*. New York: HarperCollins, 2005.

Web Links

To learn more about the San Francisco earthquake and fire, visit ABDO Publishing Company online at **www.abdopublishing.com**. Web sites about the earthquake and fire are featured on our Book Links page. These links are routinely monitored and updated to provide the most current information available. Visit **www.mycorelibrary.com** for free additional tools for teachers and students.

INDEX

ABOUT THE AUTHOR

Chrös McDougall is a reporter, author, and editor. A 2008 graduate of the University of Missouri, he has written several books for young readers on sports and history topics. He lives in the Twin Cities of Minneapolis–St. Paul with his wife.